Companion

30 DAYS TO
Unstoppable

BE THE DREAM
MADE VISIBLE

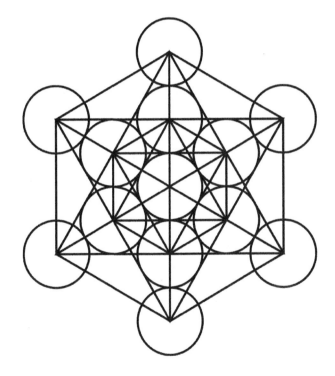

WHITNEY FREYA

FLOWER *of* LIFE PRESS

FLOWER *of* LIFE PRESS

Published by Flower of Life Press™
Old Saybrook, CT
Astara Jane Ashley, *Publisher*
floweroflifepress.com

Cover and interior design by Astara Jane Ashley
Art by Whitney Freya

Library of Congress Control Number: Available Upon Request

ISBN-13: 978-1-7371839-0-7
Printed in the United States of America

If found, please return to:

_____

_____

_____

_____

_____

Date I am beginning my **Journey to Unstoppableness**:

_____

Your Unstoppable Dream Journal

This journal has been created to support your journey to unstoppableness as inspired by BOTH the book, *30 Days to Unstoppable: Be the Dream Made Visible* and Whitney Freya's online program, "I AM the Unstoppable Dream."

The 7-Month format is intended to create significant space for you to fully integrate YOU as the union of above and below, light and matter, human being and infinite being.

The journey to "know thyself" is dependent on knowing yourself as an Infinite Being FIRST, who is SECOND having a human experience. This is your life's purpose: to remember the fullness of who you are and all you are here to create. You are an Infinite Being, embodying the form of an individual human, here to co-create new realities, inspired by love, with the Universe. When you fully integrate this truth, you become Unstoppable.

And so it is.

How to use this journal alongside the book
30 Days to Unstoppable

If you are using this companion journal alongside the book, *30 Days to Unstoppable* and are not in the online program, here are my suggestions for how to allow this journal to compliment your reading:

1. First, read the book, *30 Days to Unstoppable* from beginning to end. Then, with your full understanding of the entire Unstoppable Journey, begin your 7 month journey through the journal. As you work through the journal, you can go deeper into this meditative practice, expanding and enhancing the results you will experience in your life, referencing the book when you want to refresh your memory or receive new insights into the teaching.

2. Read through Day 6 in the book, as an introduction to the Unstoppable Journey, and, then, begin Month ONE in the journal when you start to read Day 7 "I AM the Unstoppable Dream Meditation." Each time you go to your journal, read the next chapter or two from the book. Or each time you go to read the book, also open up your journal.

This process is dynamic and will meet you where you are. Allow the book and the companion journal to be like dance partners, each bringing their own style to the "dance floor" but harmonizing together beautifully!

Contents

Monthly Prompts Explained

The 6 Spheres of Wellness

In the center of the symbol below is YOU. Surrounding you are your 6 Spheres of Wellness. Each month we get to know and fill up one of our 6 Spheres of Wellness: Love, Compassion, Courage, Alignment, Gratitude, and Presence.

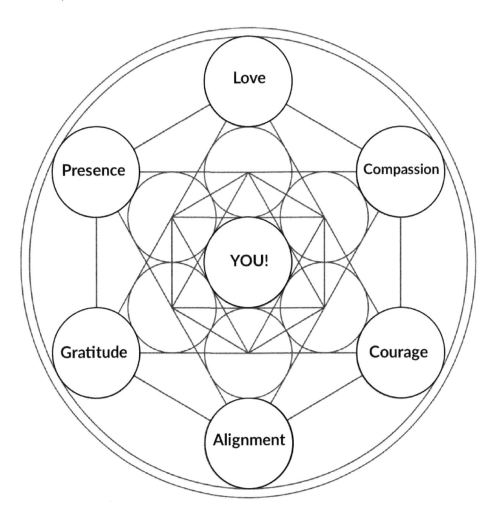

Sphere of _____

In this section, the invitation is to allow the process of automatic writing to illuminate for you the condition of your **Sphere of _____** right now. Automatic writing is when you write from a stream of consciousness, without "thinking."

You just start writing. For example:

> "This month I am exploring and filling up my Sphere of Courage. What does courage mean for me? I know it comes from the word heart. Does it involve following my heart? When I have felt courageous, I _____..."

Just write WHATEVER comes to mind.

You can also ask for your guide, your angel(s), etc. to speak to you through this writing, similar to channeling. Take a moment before you start writing to bring yourself present, breathe deeply, and ask your guide to speak to you through your writing.

Throughout the month, you are open to all the ways you can experience the energy of that sphere, all the ways you are open or closed to this energy, and to seeing any old beliefs or patterns that have blocked this energy from your life experience. For example, perhaps you feel like you acted courageously once and it didn't "work." You leaped but, from your perspective, the net did NOT appear. So you have stopped inviting in the energy of courage to create with you. You can open to letting go of that past experience. You can ask for all the little ways you can begin to dance with the energy of courage in your life.

One month at a time, you will step into your unstoppableness!

Intention for the Month

Here you can journal any kind of intentions you have for the month. It can be to organize your dresser, repeat your mantra each day, paint 4 hours a week, etc.

After Month One, you may have ah-hah's or breakthroughs from the previous month that you want to continue to integrate.

It could be that your intention for this month is to create new awareness around the language you use with yourself. Are you supportive of your dreams or not? Are you critical or open?

You may intend to get out in nature more, to sit under a tree regularly or to spend more time exercising your physical body. Anything goes here. Just remember, your intentions are powerfully creative and you want to really sink in to your intention(s) each month. Perhaps it will serve your highest good to set only one or two intentions. Let's set you up to feel fulfilled in this area at the end of each month!

And so it is.

My Mantra or Yantra for the Month

The intention of a mantra is to replace your low-vibrational mental chatter with high-vibrational words and energy. A yantra is an image or symbol that does the same thing. I love working with yantras, personally, because they do not have baggage. My yantra for my thriving biz is a hot air balloon. It reminds me to keep myself at a high vibration and share from that place. When I do, biz will thrive! The words biz, money, success, etc. can have lots of baggage while the image of the hot air balloon does not.

When we raise the vibration of our thoughts, we attract higher vibrational thoughts. The thoughts you receive at this higher vibration could be an ah-hah or other personal breakthrough, new wisdom, a fresh idea or perspective on a current idea, and much more.

You might also think of a mantra, or yantra, as a spell.

Think of the word "spelling" associated with words!

Having recently read multiple novels about witches and witchcraft, I realized that witches are extremely intentional with their words. They know their words have power. So, choose your mantra wisely. Think about the energy behind whatever you desire. For example, if you want to meet a new beloved, connect to how you want to FEEL in that relationship. Then, your mantra might be, "I AM consistently surrounded by unconditionally loving and passionate energy," or "I AM attracting to me only high vibration relationships." Even better, be the energy you desire for yourself, "I AM madly in love with my being." *Like attracts like.*

Mantras can be in your primary language or a foreign language. Yantras need no translation.

For example, one of my favorite mantras is, "Lokah Samastah Sukhino Bhavantu." This is an ancient Sanskrit prayer that communicates the essence of "May all sentient beings be happy and free and may my life in some way contribute to that happiness and freedom." What a great win-win, right?!

Another favorite is, "My life is a continuous stream of miracles." I first heard this in a song.

They can also be I AM statements, instead of, for example, "I want" or "I hope" statements.

A yantra can also be an animal totem: OWL to help me see things that I have not been able to see up until now, COYOTE to help me be a trickster in my own routines and habits, SNAKE to shed skin... It can be an ancient symbol like the ankh, the triple spiral, or sacred geometry. What you focus on expands.

And so it is.

If your desire is to have more money in your bank account, instead of saying "I AM wealthy," or "I have lots of money in my bank account," you want to say something more like, "I AM in alignment with the frequency of abundance and I experience it in all areas of my life, energetic and physical." This final version does not use any words that trigger the energy of your less-than-abundant bank account.

Or, how will you FEEL when you have more money? Is it power? Is it peace? What is a symbol that you associate with power or peace?

Another example: "I AM thin." Instead you might use, "I AM embody-ing a divine vessel that is strong and vibrant," or "I AM bathed in the energy of strength and self-love."

Enjoy the process of exploring the power of your thoughts and words. You are a powerful creator and words are your magic!

Laws of the Universe

Just as I was finishing writing *30 Days to Unstoppable*, I discovered Matias De Stefano's series on GAIA.com, called *Initiation*. In it, he explores the Laws of the Universe. Weeks later, I was guided to pick my copy of *The Emerald Tablet* from my bookshelf and I discovered that these Laws of the Universe are from the teachings of Hermes, or the Hermetic Principles. Following is a brief description of each of the laws:

Law #1: Mentalism

Thoughts become things. What you think creates your reality. This is the foundation of the Law of Mentalism, and is represented by the Crown Chakra, where you receive your call—your Unstoppable Dream—first. What you THINK about your dream, your ability to co-create it into reality with the Universe... is what will create your experience. Get quiet, close your eyes, feel into the energy of your Unstoppable You. What are your thoughts around her? These thoughts will create your experience.

Law #2: Correspondence

This law is traditionally represented by the familiar statement: "As above so below," and "As below so above." It reminds us that what we are experiencing on the "outside" of our life is a reflection of what our experience is on the "inside" of our life. If there is something going on in your life that does not have you jumping for joy, take a moment to muse on how this is also reflected within YOU. This law engages the 3rd eye chakra, allowing you to truly see and understand how what you think and feel inside corresponds to what you experience outside. Looking through this intuitive eye, what do you see about your life's experience right now?

Law #3: Vibration

Everything vibrates. Everything is energy. Vibration unifies all aspects of life, seen and unseen. Piggy backing off the Law of Correspondence, the Law of Vibration illuminates for you that if you are holding low vibratory thoughts or beliefs around anything in your life within, your experience on the outside will match that vibration. This law also connects us to our throat chakra, emphasizing that the vibration of language we use around any situation, relationship, desire, or dream will determine the vibration of our experience. Speak to the best-case scenario and you are more likely to experience that coming to fruition. Worry about failing... well, you are sending out the vibration of failure and, chances are, that is the result you will receive.

Law #4: Rhythm

The pendulum swings as far to the left as the right. The ebb and flow of the ocean reflects the ebb and flow of the Universe. What goes up, must come down. These are all reflections of the Law of Rhythm. There is a time to rest and a time to take action. Rhythm connects us to our heART chakra and the element of time. Again, inspired by vibration, the higher vibration you hold around your dream, the quicker it will come to fruition. Wondering why something you desire is taking forever to manifest? Check your vibration around your desire. Do you follow up your desire with frustration (low vibration) that it hasn't happened yet? Or do you follow up your desire with all the ways it can come into your reality (high vibration)? Also, when we are operating at a higher vibration, life's lessons can be experienced and learned quicker, at a faster rhythm, than if we are living at a lower vibration. Think of how you move and feel differently to fast paced music as opposed to slooooowwww music. Both are great, but generate very different experiences. Which experience do you choose?

Law #5: Cause & Effect

There is a cause for every experience and an effect of every experience. This law reminds us that we are the only ones responsible for our life experience. It corresponds to the solar plexus chakra—your personal power and will. It encourages us to believe that nothing in our life experience is without a purpose. What is the effect you desire? How can you cause it? What is an effect you are experiencing (regardless of whether it is low or high vibration) and how did you cause it? The opposite is slipping into the victim mentality or the "waiting for my ship to come in" story. This can be a difficult mirror to look into, AND way more productive than trying to bypass this principle. It can inform you as you take steps forward in the creative process of life!

Law #6: Polarity

Everything has a positive and a negative, a dark and a light, and one helps to create the other. Polarity is a creative force (as represented by your sacral or 2nd chakra) and can often be misinterpreted as a force of separation or an obstacle. "Necessity is the mother of invention" is an old saying that mirrors the principle of polarity. When things in life aren't working, that non-working energy is there to inspire you to shift, to change, to pivot. Is something not going the way you expected, perhaps for the worse? Instead of camping out in the energy of disappointment, this law invites you to allow this "dark" to turn your vision towards the "light." The negative is there to inform you and guide you into the positive. Think about what you have to do first if you are going to jump UP. You first have to crouch down, right? How can you allow ALL of your experience—the pleasurable and the unpleasurable—to guide and inform you?

Law #7: Generation (or Gender)

This speaks to the truth that everything is creative. Everything is here to create. The ROOT (chakra) of all existence is creative, generative. Everything has a masculine and a feminine SO that it can align with the creative energy of the Universe. Life is not meant to be stagnant. You are meant to continuously experience change. It is how you learn, grow, and expand. This principle also speaks to the dance between creation and destruction. Creation always follows destruction. Trying to resist change, to resist the creative nature of the Universe, will only frustrate you or attract to you whatever it takes to get you into creative energy. There is nothing in your life that isn't wanting to facilitate the generation of newness. Reflect on what creating, creativity, and creation mean to you. Which moments in your life have inspired your creativity? In Cyndi Dale's book, *The Complete Book of Chakra Healing*, she writes that we are only here to heal and to create.

And so it is.

Everything about the experience of 30 Days to Unstoppable is intended to bring you into coherence with the highest vibrations you have available to you right now. So, overlaying the 7 Laws of the Universe onto the Unstoppable Journey is the perfect compliment.

When we try to create the life of our dreams without the full cooperation of the Universe, we are going to be struggling against a very strong current. Likewise, when we shift into alignment with these laws, your life can unfold in unprecedented FLOW.

Each month in this journal, you will focus on just one of the Laws of the Universe. You will see how they all build upon and compliment one another.

Regardless of your human experience up until now, you can transform any aspect of your life when you allow your infinite awareness to co-create with the full power and energy of the Universe.

These laws are simple, but not easy. Be gentle with yourself while choosing to align with these principles. You can remove your attention from the way things have been up until now and redirect it with a committed focus towards that which you feel called to experience—and all the ways you will be supported—until its fruition.

Notice where you meet up with resistance.

Resistance is energy showing us where we are not in coherence with the Laws of the Universe, where our vibration is low. Ask the resistance, "WHY? What do I fear if I fully integrate this law? Whose voice is in my head telling me this is 'hogwash?' What do I want now?"

Because what you really, really, really want is also what the Universe wants. Surrender to this infinite source of inspiration, support, wisdom and strength and watch the transformation unfold before you.

And so it is.

P.S. Search "The 7 Hermetic Principles" for oodles of resources to supplement your experience (especially if you are not in the online program at WhitneyFreyaStudio.com). The order of the principles that I use is sourced from Matias de Stefano's series on GAIA.com, "Initiation." I highly recommend this series as well!

All the ways I am in coherence:

What we focus on expands. This is a beautiful truth... unless we are allowing our focus to direct our attention towards those things we don't want.

Coherence is when your focus and attention is pointed in the direction of what you desire. Imagine you are holding a bow and arrow. Now imagine the target. Is that target a new home, new job, new relationship, new level of physical wellness, etc? Now, if you want to hit that target, do you want to point your arrow directly at the target? If you aim your arrow 5 yards the right of the target or 5 yards under the target, will you hit it? No.

Coherence is when every cell of your being, every word in your head, every sentence you utter out loud is in alignment with your desire. You ARE the bow and the arrow and the huntress aiming with everything available to you at the "bullseye."

In this section, list all the ways you are in coherence. If you want a new job, you may write things like:

- I am open to accepting a new job that I love.
- I am actively reaching out to learn about new career opportunities.
- I am making the most of where I am working now, doing my best so that I am in alignment with thriving in any work environment.
- I am...

These musings may lead to new understanding about ways you can take new action to create greater coherence around your desire or dream.

And so it is.

All the ways I am being given opportunities to shift into coherence:

We often learn best through contrast. Perhaps your "target" is to create a more physically fit physical body. Maybe you find yourself succumbing to that bowl of ice cream after dinner or skipping exercise time.

Instead of beating yourself up, recognize that some of the choices you have made are not in coherence with your desire. Now you know how that feels and you want to choose otherwise.

For example, instead of "I haven't done yoga in weeks" creating a barrage of self-criticism, you can counter with: "I must be coming up on a yoga cycle." Your awareness that you have NOT done something can direct your focus towards that which you DO want to do.

Perhaps your focus is on honoring or deepening your meditation practice. Maybe your meditations have been interrupted lately by a family member or phone calls. Now you understand that you want to choose to meditate in a more private space or let your household know that you won't be available for a bit. And you now remember to turn off your ringer. Instead of spiraling into a vortex of "I can't do this," or "This isn't working for me," you can allow your experience up until now to redirect your focus back towards your target with greater conviction and alignment.

And so it is.

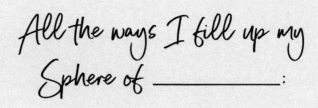

All the ways I fill up my Sphere of _____:

This is another space to use automatic writing to collect as many different ways you can fill up each month on the energy of love, compassion, courage, alignment, gratitude, and presence.

Here, you are encouraged to explore the energy of the month from as many facets as possible. For example, what are all the things that you love? ...that you love to do? ...love to eat? ...people you love? ...images, animals, colors...that inspire the feeling of love? ...that you love about mornings? ...that you love about sunset? ...that you love about winter? ...summer? ...that you love about yourself? ...that you love about the way you _____ ? What are all the SIMPLE things you love? ...the smell of pine needles in the warm sunlight? ...dark chocolate? ...that pillow on your bed?

Again, what we focus on expands. Exploring ALL the sources of these energies will only attract greater awareness. Add to this list throughout the month, re-committing to your focus each time.

And so it is.

What I have learned from the aspect of me who _____ :

Remember the aspect of you who was 21 years old? Or remember the aspect of you that used to care SO much about what others thought? When you do this, you are remembering, connecting with, the "you" that is in the past. Likewise, you can "remember" or connect with the aspect of you that is in the future, doing or experiencing what is right now the seed of this vision.

You are remembering into your future, rather than remembering into your past.

Imagine the "you" that is in complete and total coherence with your heart's desire. What does this aspect of you have to share right now?

If your focus is on stepping into a new career, imagine you are sitting down to coffee with the "you" that is already embodying this new career. You and she are meeting after work. What advice does she have for you right now?

This process is taught in my online program, "I AM the Unstoppable Dream." It compliments your journey to unstoppableness so perfectly.

When you receive an Unstoppable Dream, you can connect to the aspect of you that has already brought it to fruition and ask her for tips and insight.

Time is not linear. You can "remember your future." You do this when you worry—you imagine into a future that you don't like. Let's flip that and imagine into a future that makes your heart sing, imagine yourself already there, experiencing it, and ask this aspect of you what very next step to take.

You are wiser than you have imagined up until now. Now you harness your imagination to choose a future experience and to guide you there along your highest path.

And so it is.

My highest vision for my life right now that also benefits all sentient beings:

Where are you feeling not enough?

What is worrying you?

What is generating fear in your life?

Where do you feel wobbly?

Now, how many other people on this planet do you imagine might be feeling this way as well? How would you want them to feel? What are all the ways you can generate that feeling for yourself and, then, ripple that out so that all sentient beings benefit?

These low vibration musings are in your awareness so that you can transform them into high vibration musings.

What would it feel like to be more than enough?

What would be the best possible future scenario?

What is wanting to be loved?

What is wanting to be strengthened?

Maybe you have been feeling alone. Do you think there are others on this planet also feeling the energies of loneliness? How would you want for them to feel? Connected? Supported? What are all the ways you can create opportunities for yoursef to feel more connected and supported? Can you ask for help? Can you reach out to a friend or a community? Can you share something you love with someone? Can you offer a favor?

You ARE the change you want to see in the world.

And so it is.

My vision for my eARTh:

This is a similar experience as the last one, but the focus is even *more* on the collective.

You can connect to a part of the planet, or a situation, or a country... that generates negative or low vibrations within you. What aspect of our eARTh causes the most discordance for you right now? And what are all the ways you can send it coherent, loving, or compassionate energies in that direction?

Since everything is energy, when so many humans are sending negative energy towards a certain area or a person, it becomes harder and harder to change the momentum of energy from downward to upward. We can send love where we might normally find ourselves sending hate or judgment—and all sentient beings will benefit.

And so it is.

Symbols that support me this month:

The creative universal energies wanting to flow through you and co-create your Unstoppable Dreams with you, speak a different language than your rational, logical mind. Symbols are a magical and powerful form of communication on your journey to your unstoppableness!

This is a space to collect your symbols that are being offered to you to provide energy that will support your high vibration and coherence with your Unstoppable Dream.

A symbol can be a plant, animal or thing.

You are made aware of these symbols through repetition or energy. You might be seeing butterflies everywhere, so this is a symbol. Or, you might get super stoked at the first glimpse of a lotus flower or an owl.

You are guided to receive the gift of a symbol in each of your Unstoppable Dream meditations. The future aspect of you who has already experienced the fruition of your Unstoppable Dream can give you a gift, a symbol that will remind you of "her," of the future you that is already there.

You might also take a moment in this prompt to think back to your childhood, or another time in your past, and remember what you collected, or what a visual theme was in your life. For example, I associate my entire childhood with strawberries. My bedroom always had a big strawberry theme and I, therefore, attracted gifts that included strawberry images. When I was looking up plants associated with the Goddess Freya, I found that the strawberry plant was one of them!

You may find yourself painting a certain shape over and over again on your canvas, or being attracted to jewelry with a particular crystal or stone. These are also powerful symbols.

You can also look up symbols that connect to what you desire more of in your life this month. What is a symbol for patience (the caterpillar or cocoon perhaps)? What about a symbol to help deepen your meditation (the whale)?

Use these symbols as you meditate. Paint them onto your canvas or draw them in this journal. Allow them to show up differently in your mind's eye each time. This is how they meet you exactly where you are in that moment. Symbols have been around much longer than written language and need no translation. Makes sense that your Infinite Self would communicate in this manner, right?

You are receiving more and more guidance and affirmation through the symbols that are speaking to you each day.

And so it is.

What if...

In Day 30 of the book, we are encouraged to ask the question "What if..." as part of "Your Daily Practice." In this section of the companion journal, you can record your "What if's..." How fun will it be to look back at the What if's that come to fruition?!

Unstoppable Dream Templates

You can create your own personalized Unstoppable Dream templates for unique elements in your life such as your business, marriage, role as a parent, or health. What are the Six Spheres of Wellness for your role as a mother, leader, or business owner? A client of mine used the template to create a product of her's into her own Unstoppable Dream! She wrote the product in the center of Metatron's Cube and then added her own energies into the Six Spheres: intuition, trust, abundance, truth, presence, and love. With those six energies focused upon and emphasized in the creation and marketing of her product, she felt like it would be Unstoppable! And it helped her focus her energies. You could even use the templates for a family vacation, a retreat you are offering—or attending! Maybe you are entering into a specific life experience such as moving, healing, marrying, divorcing, or learning something new. These are just some examples! Have fun with this!

Unstoppable Dream Calendar

Document a year in the life of your unstoppableness! This is a dateless calendar, so add in the month and date for each calendar. So regardless of when you start, you have a 12-month calendar to capture the magical moments of your journey to Unstoppable!

Here are some ideas for how to use this calendar:

- Use this calendar to keep track of your day to day activities, and create more reasons to spend time with this journal.

- Document your ah-hah's and Unstoppable Dreams as you receive them in the appropriate date. Then you can look back to witness your journey to unstoppableness!

- When you receive an Unstoppable Dream, vision into its fruition and write down your intentions, benchmarks, and goals in the appropriate dates to help hold you accountable.

- In the section underneath the monthly calendar, capture the synchronicities and coincidences that will absolutely increase in frequency the more you tune into YOU as the Unstoppable Dream. The more energy you give to these magical moments, the more they will show up!

Unstoppable Dream Calendar

Month   Year

sunday	monday	tuesday	wednesday	thursday	friday	saturday

My Unstoppable Synchronicities & Coincidences

_____   _____

_____   _____

_____   _____

_____   _____

_____   _____

_____   _____

_____   _____

Month   Year

sunday	monday	tuesday	wednesday	thursday	friday	saturday

My Unstoppable Synchronicities & Coincidences

_____   _____

_____   _____

_____   _____

_____   _____

_____   _____

_____   _____

Setting Your Intention

DATE _____

Introduction to the Unstoppable Dream Meditation

To listen to the Unstoppable Dream Meditation, visit my YouTube channel and listen to Day SEVEN in the 30 Days to Unstoppable audio/video book: https://youtu.be/7ditMkdwDN4.

Allow yourself time and space here for automatic writing around the Unstoppable Dream Meditation. What does the symbol of Metatron's Cube inspire? How do the Spheres of Wellness feel? Which sphere stands out the most for you? Why? Allow your pen to just write...

My *Intention* for the MONTH:

What is your intention for this month? Where do you want to experience change? Fill in this space (perhaps multiple times throughout the month) to reflect on why you are here and what you are being called into.

My *Mantra or Yantra* for the MONTH:

Which words or symbols vibrate with your desire for this month? Again, you can come back to this section throughout the month. Imagine you are getting to know this new practice more and more as the month progresses. Write (and draw) about it below.

Law of the Universe: **MENTALISM**

Thoughts become things. This is the foundation of the Law of Mentalism. This is the Crown Chakra, where you receive your call, your Unstoppable Dream first. What you THINK about your dream, your ability to co-create it into reality with the Universe... is what will create your experience. Get quiet, close your eyes, feel into the energy of your Unstoppable You. What are your thoughts around her? These thoughts will create your experience. Journal here about the thoughts you are now choosing to think.

All the ways I am in coherence:

This is where you express your own inner cheerleader! This can be a series of I AM... statements in which you are making present moment statements as if you are already realizing the fruition of your dreams or desires. What are all the ways you are poised and ready for your unstoppableness? Write about it below.

All the ways I am being given opportunities to shift into coherence:

Anywhere you are experiencing the energy of struggle or frustration etc. is where you are being given an opportunity to shift that part or element of your life into coherence. Instead of beating yourself up, you are choosing to illuminate all the opportunities you are being offered in the situation. Write about it below.

Unstoppable Dream Meditation

Reflect this month on your "Energetic Noah's Ark." What are your first impressions of this process? Where is there resonance? Where do you wonder? What do you feel is possible with a deepening into this energetic space around and within you?
Write about it below.

What I have learned from the aspect of me who _____:

In my online course, "I AM the Unstoppable Dream," you learn how to remember into your future. You imagine your desired future and you imagine yourself there, experiencing the fruition of your dream, and then ask this future YOU for advice, words of wisdom, or guidance in the present moment. Imagine the YOU that is surrounded by an expansive energy field infused with the Six Spheres of Wellness. What are you doing differently? How do you feel different? What changes have occurred as a result? Write about it below.

My highest vision for my life right now:

Dream into your highest vision for this month. Expand upon it below. Bathe yourself in best case scenarios, dreams coming true, miracles and synchronicities abounding...
And so it is!

My vision for my eARTh:

This is the space in which you dedicate your own practice this month to the benefit of all humanity. Perhaps you write a prayer here or a mantra for our world. Perhaps you pick an element of life on this planet (environment, children, peace...) and describe your vision as if it is already happening.

Symbols that support me this month:

In the mantra and yantra section you received words and/or a symbol to guide you this month. Here, recognize the symbols that showed up in all the ways they can to support, encourage, and inspire you this month. Maybe this moment will be the first time you recognize how a symbol has repeated itself or how a symbol has really attracted you. It could be a color, an animal, element of nature, or a more traditional symbol. Write and draw about it below.

What if...

Start a journal entry below with these two words. Pay attention as you see where it leads you. In the space following those two words, at the perfect moment, you will meet your next Unstoppable Dream.

Month 2

Month   Year

sunday	monday	tuesday	wednesday	thursday	friday	saturday

My Unstoppable Synchronicities & Coincidences

Sphere of Love

DATE _____

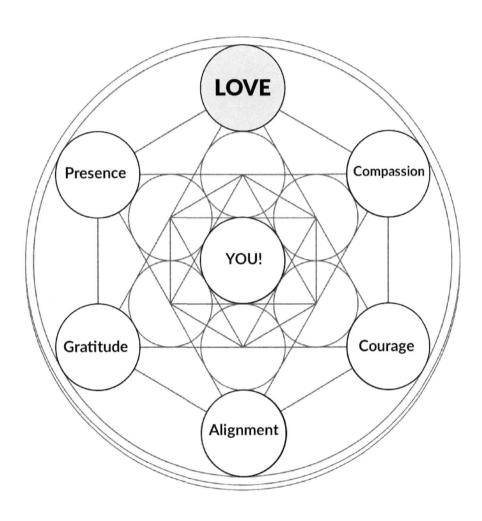

My *Intention* for the MONTH:

My *Mantra or Yantra* for the MONTH:

Law of the Universe: CORRESPONDENCE

This law is traditionally represented by the familiar statement: "As above so below," and "As below so above." It reminds us that what we are experiencing on the "outside" of our life is a reflection of what our experience is on the "inside" of our life. If there is something going on in your life that does not have you jumping for joy, take a moment to muse on how this is also reflected within YOU. This law engages the 3rd eye chakra, allowing you to truly see and understand how what you think and feel inside corresponds to what you experience outside. Looking through this intuitive eye, what do you see about your life's experience right now? Write about it below.

All the ways I am in coherence:

All the ways I am being given opportunities to shift into coherence:

All the ways I fill up my Sphere of _____ :

What I have learned from the aspect of me who:

My highest vision for my life right now:

My vision for my eARTh:

Symbols that support me this month:

What if...

Month

Year

sunday	monday	tuesday	wednesday	thursday	friday	saturday

My Unstoppable Synchronicities & Coincidences

_____   _____
_____   _____
_____   _____
_____   _____
_____   _____
_____   _____

Sphere of Compassion

DATE ——————————

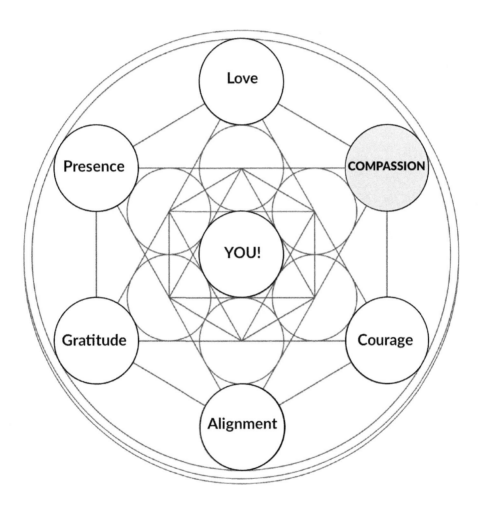

My *Intention* for the MONTH:

My *Mantra or Yantra* for the MONTH:

Law of the Universe: **VIBRATION**

Everything vibrates. Everything is energy. Vibration unifies all aspects of life, seen and unseen. Piggy backing off the Law of Correspondence, the Law of Vibration illuminates for you that if you are holding low vibratory thoughts or beliefs around anything in your life within, your experience on the outside will match that vibration. This law also connects us to our throat chakra, emphasizing that the vibration of language we use around any situation, relationship, desire, or dream will determine the vibration of our experience. Speak to the best-case scenario and you are more likely to experience that coming to fruition. Worry about failing... well, you are sending out the vibration of failure and, chances are, that is the result you will receive.

All the ways I am in coherence:

All the ways I am being given opportunities to shift into coherence:

All the ways I fill up my Sphere of _____:

What I have learned from the aspect of me who:

My highest vision for my life right now:

My vision for my eARTh:

Symbols that support me this month:

What if...

Month

Year

sunday	monday	tuesday	wednesday	thursday	friday	saturday

My Unstoppable Synchronicities & Coincidences

_____   _____
_____   _____
_____   _____
_____   _____
_____   _____
_____   _____

Sphere of Courage

DATE _____

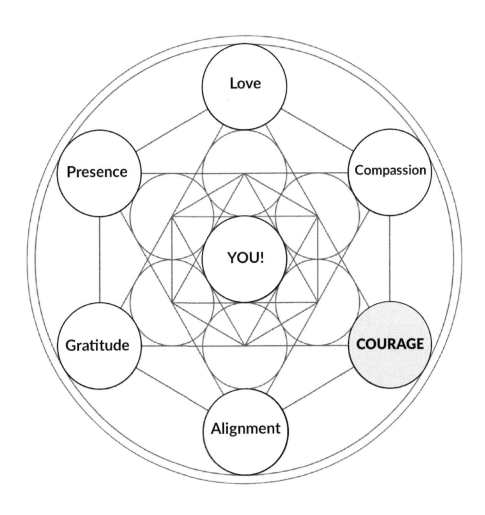

My *Intention* for the MONTH:

My *Mantra or Yantra* for the MONTH:

Law of the Universe: **RHYTHM**

The pendulum swings as far to the left as the right. The ebb and flow of the ocean reflects the ebb and flow of the Universe. What goes up, must come down. These are all reflections of the Law of Rhythm. There is a time to rest and a time to take action. Rhythm connects us to our heART chakra and the element of time. Again, inspired by vibration, the higher vibration you hold around your dream, the quicker it will come to fruition. Wondering why something you desire is taking forever to manifest? Check your vibration around your desire. Do you follow up your desire with frustration (low vibration) that it hasn't happened yet? Or do you follow up your desire with all the ways it can come into your reality (high vibration)? Also, when we are operating at a higher vibration, life's lessons can be experienced and learned quicker, at a faster rhythm, than if we are living at a lower vibration. Think of how you move and feel differently to fast paced music as opposed to slooooowwww music. Both are great, but generate very different experiences. Which experience do you choose? Write about it below.

All the ways I am in coherence:

All the ways I am being given opportunities to shift into coherence:

All the ways I fill up my Sphere of _____:

What I have learned from the aspect of me who:

My highest vision for my life right now:

My vision for my eARTh:

Symbols that support me this month:

What if...

Month 5

Month

Year

sunday	monday	tuesday	wednesday	thursday	friday	saturday

My Unstoppable Synchronicities & Coincidences

_____   _____
_____   _____
_____   _____
_____   _____
_____   _____
_____   _____
_____   _____

Sphere of Alignment

DATE _____

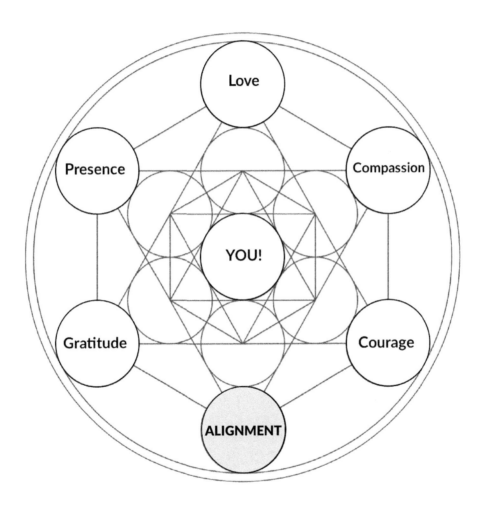

My *Intention* for the MONTH:

My *Mantra or Yantra* for the MONTH:

Law of the Universe: CAUSE & EFFECT

There is a cause for every experience and an effect of every experience. This law reminds us that we are the only ones responsible for our life experience. It corresponds to the solar plexus chakra—your personal power and will. It encourages us to believe that nothing in our life experience is without a purpose. What is the effect you desire? How can you cause it? What is an effect you are experiencing (regardless of whether it is low or high vibration) and how did you cause it? The opposite is slipping into the victim mentality or the "waiting for my ship to come in" story. This can be a difficult mirror to look into, AND way more productive than trying to bypass this principle. It can inform you as you take steps forward in the creative process of life!

All the ways I am in coherence:

All the ways I am being given opportunities to shift into coherence:

All the ways I fill up my Sphere of _____:

What I have learned from the aspect of me who:

My highest vision for my life right now:

My vision for my eARTh:

Symbols that support me this month:

What if...

Month 6

Month   Year

sunday	monday	tuesday	wednesday	thursday	friday	saturday

My Unstoppable Synchronicities & Coincidences

_____   _____
_____   _____
_____   _____
_____   _____
_____   _____
_____   _____

Sphere of Gratitude

DATE _____

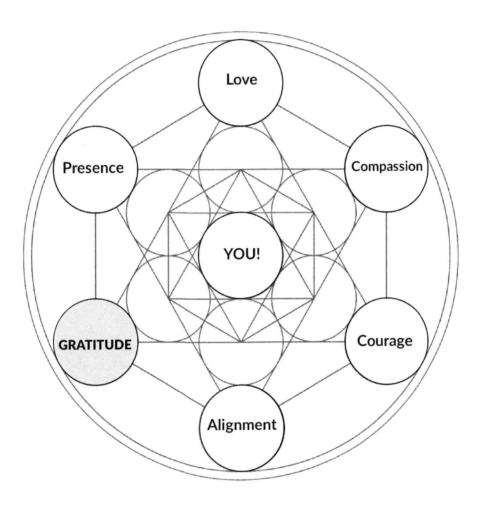

My *Intention* for the MONTH:

My Mantra or Yantra for the MONTH:

Law of the Universe: POLARITY

Everything has a positive and a negative, a dark and a light, and one helps to create the other. Polarity is a creative force (as represented by your sacral or 2nd chakra) and can often be misinterpreted as a force of separation or an obstacle. "Necessity is the mother of invention" is an old saying that mirrors the principle of polarity. When things in life aren't working, that non-working energy is there to inspire you to shift, to change, to pivot. Is something not going the way you expected, perhaps for the worse? Instead of camping out in the energy of disappointment, this law invites you to allow this "dark" to turn your vision towards the "light." The negative is there to inform you and guide you into the positive. Think about what you have to do first if you are going to jump UP. You first have to crouch down, right? How can you allow ALL of your experience—the pleasurable and the unpleasurable—to guide and inform you?

All the ways I am in coherence:

All the ways I am being given opportunities to shift into coherence:

All the ways I fill up my Sphere of _____:

What I have learned from the aspect of me who:

My highest vision for my life right now:

My vision for my eARTh:

Symbols that support me this month:

What if...

Month 7

Month   Year

sunday	monday	tuesday	wednesday	thursday	friday	saturday

My Unstoppable Synchronicities & Coincidences

_____ _____
_____ _____
_____ _____
_____ _____
_____ _____
_____ _____

Sphere of Presence

DATE _____

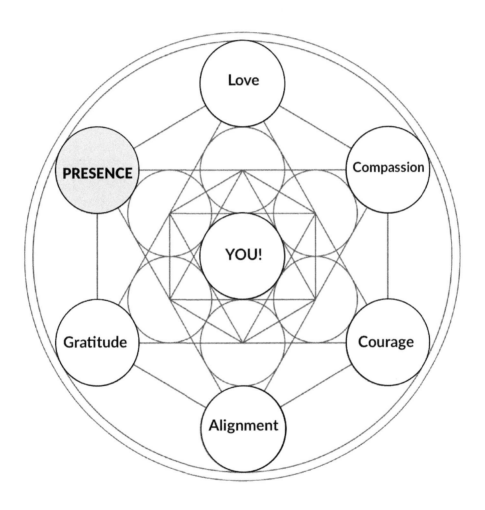

My *Intention* for the MONTH:

My *Mantra* or *Yantra* for the MONTH:

Law of the Universe: GENERATION

This speaks to the truth that everything is creative. Everything is here to create. The ROOT (chakra) of all existence is creative, generative. Everything has a masculine and a feminine SO that it can align with the creative energy of the Universe. Life is not meant to be stagnant. You are meant to continuously experience change. It is how you learn, grow, and expand. This principle also speaks to the dance between creation and destruction. Creation always follows destruction. Trying to resist change, to resist the creative nature of the Universe, will only frustrate you or attract to you whatever it takes to get you into creative energy. There is nothing in your life that isn't wanting to facilitate the generation of newness. Reflect on what creating, creativity, and creation mean to you. Which moments in your life have inspired your creativity? In Cyndi Dale's book, The Complete Book of Chakra Healing, she writes that we are only here to heal and to create.

All the ways I am in coherence:

All the ways I am being given opportunities to shift into coherence:

All the ways I fill up my Sphere of _____:

What I have learned from the aspect of me who:

My highest vision for my life right now:

My vision for my eARTh:

Symbols that support me this month:

What if...

Conclusion

Your journey into your most unstoppable nature is a never ending one. You will simply become more and more unstoppable!

Thank you for capturing your musings, celebrations, and reflections on the previous pages. May this journal continue to create space for your personal expansion into the fullness of who you are.

On the following pages are 12 monthly calendars, so you can continue to use this journal starting now for the year ahead. Following that are the templates that you can use to create your own Metatron's Cube of unstoppableness for different projects, relationships, or products you want to create. Instead of writing "YOU" in the center sphere, write the subject that is wanting to be unstoppable. In each of the six spheres, write the same themes we have explored in this journal or receive your own combination of energies that will guide whatever you have placed in the center into its own unstoppable nature.

YOU are an Infinite Being here to create from your heART. May this journal and accompanying book remind you of all the magic and resources you have at your fingertips. I honor you and your journey and all the wild and lovely dreams swirling around you!

YOU are unstoppable!

And so it is.

~Whitney Freya

Unstoppable Dream Calendar

Month   Year

sunday	monday	tuesday	wednesday	thursday	friday	saturday

My Unstoppable Synchronicities & Coincidences

_____   _____

_____   _____

_____   _____

_____   _____

_____   _____

_____   _____

_____   _____

Unstoppable Dream Calendar

Month   ## Year

sunday	monday	tuesday	wednesday	thursday	friday	saturday

My Unstoppable Synchronicities & Coincidences

_____   _____
_____   _____
_____   _____
_____   _____
_____   _____
_____   _____
_____   _____
_____   _____

Unstoppable Dream Calendar

Month   ## Year

sunday	monday	tuesday	wednesday	thursday	friday	saturday

My Unstoppable Synchronicities & Coincidences

Unstoppable Dream Calendar

Month   Year

sunday	monday	tuesday	wednesday	thursday	friday	saturday

My Unstoppable Synchronicities & Coincidences

_____   _____
_____   _____
_____   _____
_____   _____
_____   _____
_____   _____
_____   _____

Unstoppable Dream Calendar

Month   Year

sunday	monday	tuesday	wednesday	thursday	friday	saturday

My Unstoppable Synchronicities & Coincidences

_____   _____

_____   _____

_____   _____

_____   _____

_____   _____

_____   _____

_____   _____

Unstoppable Dream Calendar

Month   Year

sunday	monday	tuesday	wednesday	thursday	friday	saturday

My Unstoppable Synchronicities & Coincidences

_____   _____

_____   _____

_____   _____

_____   _____

_____   _____

_____   _____

_____   _____

Unstoppable Dream Calendar

Month   Year

sunday	monday	tuesday	wednesday	thursday	friday	saturday

My Unstoppable Synchronicities & Coincidences

_____   _____
_____   _____
_____   _____
_____   _____
_____   _____
_____   _____
_____   _____
_____   _____

Unstoppable Dream Calendar

Month   Year

sunday	monday	tuesday	wednesday	thursday	friday	saturday

My Unstoppable Synchronicities & Coincidences

_____ _____

_____ _____

_____ _____

_____ _____

_____ _____

_____ _____

_____ _____

Unstoppable Dream Calendar

Month

Year

sunday	monday	tuesday	wednesday	thursday	friday	saturday

My Unstoppable Synchronicities & Coincidences

_____   _____
_____   _____
_____   _____
_____   _____
_____   _____
_____   _____
_____   _____

Unstoppable Dream Calendar

Month   Year

sunday	monday	tuesday	wednesday	thursday	friday	saturday

My Unstoppable Synchronicities & Coincidences

_____   _____
_____   _____
_____   _____
_____   _____
_____   _____
_____   _____
_____   _____
_____   _____

Unstoppable Dream Calendar

Month   Year

sunday	monday	tuesday	wednesday	thursday	friday	saturday

My Unstoppable Synchronicities & Coincidences

_____   _____
_____   _____
_____   _____
_____   _____
_____   _____
_____   _____
_____   _____
_____   _____